DESPERATELY SEEKING
Van Gogh

IAN CASTELLO-CORTES

GINGKO PRESS

Early Years

Genius emerges in the most unexpected places. In Vincent's case it was from a dull, windswept, poor and featureless village in the Netherlands, Zundert, close to the Belgian border. This was where Theodorus (known as Dorus) and Anna Van Gogh, a Protestant pastor and his wife, settled in 1851. Both were from upper middle class families in sophisticated The Hague. Dorus's four older brothers pursued careers in business, the armed forces and the civil service. It fell on Dorus to follow his father into the Church, albeit, unlike his father, who liked his luxuries, in poor parishes. He might not have been Anna Carbentus's ideal match, but, turning 30, she was under pressure to marry. Dorus became a strict, upstanding leader to his congregation, and a caring if slightly distant father, whilst Anna made it her life's work to project bourgeois respectability. In 1852, on March 30th, Anna gave birth to a stillborn baby, whom she and Dorus named Vincent. Exactly a year later she gave birth to a second boy, whom the Van Goghs also named Vincent, steadily followed by Vincent's siblings: Anna (1855), Theodorus ('Theo', 1857), Elisabeth ('Lies', 1859), Willemina ('Wil', 1862) and Cornelis ('Cor', 1867). Vincent felt an intense attachment to his mother. What she, who had a reputation for being cold, felt about Vincent, as he grew into an odd, withdrawn and difficult child, is undocumented. But many years later she did reflect that she was "never so busy as when we only had Vincent."

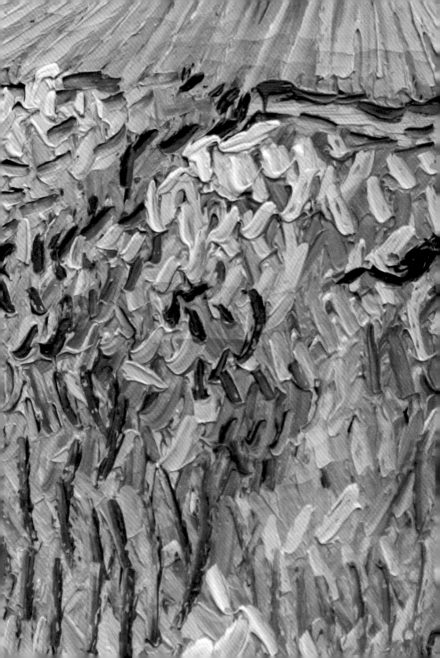

1

ZUNDERT

"Those were happy years, back then in Zundert!" Lies (Vincent's sister).

For Vincent Van Gogh, born in the parsonage in Zundert, in 1853, the somewhat bleak village was always home. Anna, his mother, had created a powerful sense of devotion to family, which Vincent from an early age took intensely to heart. The parsonage rather took on the aspect of a ship in a storm – a civilised protestant outpost in a sea of Catholic superstition, illiteracy and ignorance. Anna's pride and joy was the garden she created, where she schooled her children in the detailed wonders of nature. After family dinners, Dorus loved to delve into family history, followed by readings from sentimental authors such as Dickens, Beecher Stowe and Bulwer-Lytton. Of all the many celebrations throughout the year, Christmas held an exalted place. Yet the wonders of family did not always mean warmth or ease. For the Van Goghs, and their children, upstanding behaviour in the village, discipline and presenting a pukka, well-dressed and ordered face to the World were paramount. For the intensely emotional, reclusive Vincent the sense that love and family were contingent on sticking to social rules was to prove an extremely difficult and deeply damaging challenge. It would colour his whole life.

WHERE?
COUNTRY PATH,
ZUNDERT OUTSKIRTS.

②

THE CREEKBANK

"I adored him more than anything imaginable." **Theo, about Vincent**

By any measure Vincent was a rather difficult child. He was prone to intense temper tantrums. He was a contrarian – whatever the course of action he was asked to follow, he opted for the opposite. Villagers commented on the 'strange boy' from the parsonage – mortifying for Anna. Finding interactions with humans difficult, Vincent found his escape in nature, specifically in a stream and its banks in the fields beyond the house. Here Vincent would sit for hours observing the water bugs, nesting birds, flowers and roots. He loved to go out in storms and at night. As the family expanded, Vincent played with his siblings, but only stayed close to Theo, born when Vincent was four. They shared adventures along the creekbank, shared a bed and Vincent loved teaching Theo all he knew. But they were such different characters. Where Vincent was withdrawn, Theo was sociable. Where Vincent was obtuse, Theo was helpful. Anna soon made her favouritism clear: "my angelic Theo", she called him. Vincent became more withdrawn as a result.

WHAT?
CLOSELY OBSERVED GRASS,
BY VINCENT.

3

ZEVENBERGEN

"What beautiful days..." Lies (sister), on Vincent's return from the Provily school.

As Theo's star rose in the family, so Vincent's fell. He started going on solitary walks, walking out of the house in silence. He began reading intense romantic novelists who revelled in lonely redemption through nature. He began to collect flowers, eggs and bugs obsessively. Schooling was not a success. Anna and Dorus sent Vincent to the local public school, then home schooled him for three years with a governess. Vincent was bored out of his tree. In despair, his parents then decided on boarding school: the Provily School in Zevenbergen. Vincent felt only loneliness and abandonment. He felt cast adrift from a family that would now become closer without him. Occasional visits from Dorus sent him into a state of despair; there are no records of Anna having visited. Letters home spoke of his manic unhappiness. Finally, after two years, Dorus and Anna relented: a new boarding school, they thought, would be the answer. Anything but having Vincent at home.

WHERE?
THE PROVILY SCHOOL,
ZEVENBERGEN.

(4)

TILBURG

"Sketch the impression the object makes, not the object itself." **Constantin Husymans, Tilburg schoolmaster.**

The Willem II School at Tilburg was more impressive than the Provily School, and further away, but it did offer a great array of courses taught by a clever faculty. It made zero impression on Vincent. In more than 1000 letters in later life he never mentioned his time there, not even the excellent art teaching. Vincent treated the experience as another forced exile, and made no attempt at forging friendships. His classmates showed little interest in the strange country boy who boarded with a couple in their late fifties, whilst they all went home to their families. Hard-faced Anna again never visited, and the distance made it harder for Dorus. Trips home highlighted how Vincent was becoming estranged from his four siblings. When he absconded a few days before his fifteenth birthday and walked all the way home, he was grudgingly accepted back at the parsonage. Anna worried about the shame it would bring on the family, who were meant to lead by example. Dorus fretted about the wasted expense. But Vincent was home. This frenetic search for love and home was to be a regular pattern for the rest of his life.

⑤

UNCLE CENT

"Everything gets sold."
Uncle Cent's business moto

Vincent's art dealer uncle – Dorus's brother – was the stand-out success of the family. Also called Vincent, but known as Cent, he and his wife, Anna's sister, could not have children. They lived in a splendid mansion in The Hague, before moving to a stunning *haut bourgeois* apartment in Paris. The source of Cent Van Gogh's wealth was an art print dealership, which had started modestly enough as an artists' supplies shop on The Hague's Spuistraat. Cent latched onto a growing bourgeois taste for high-grade art reproductions just as the fashion was kicking off, and business grew fast. The key to success was to treat art as a marketable commodity, to anticipate the public's taste and then to be quick to supply it at the right price. Cent's company, now named The Van Gogh International Art Dealership, became hugely profitable, to the point where, in 1861, aged 40, he achieved a coup by forming a partnership with Goupil, the market leaders in Paris. For Dorus and Anna a light went on: what if the fatherless Cent could take young Vincent under his wing and make something useful of him?

WHERE?
GOUPIL & CIE,
2 PLACE DE L'OPÉRA,
1ST ARRONDISSEMENT,
PARIS.

6

THE HAGUE

"I am very busy and glad of it,...for that is what I want." Vincent to Theo

It took 16 months for Vincent to be persuaded to accept Cent's open offer of a position at the renamed Goupil & Cie. There was screaming frustration at the parsonage. What was wrong with Vincent that he preferred endless solitary walks and bug collecting to earning a useful living? But once he'd decided Vincent plunged into the job in his usual obsessive fashion. He worked hard, sharpened his wardrobe, and at first became close to his boss, Hermanus Gijsbertus Tersteeg ('HG'). Vincent devoured books on artists, and his time sorting and packaging images allowed him to absorb a multiplicity of styles in the Goupil catalogue in double-quick time. He was across new movements in art, particularly the Barbizon School, the English pre-Raphaelites and the Dutch Romantics. After a few years, Goupil decided to allow him to deal directly with clients, and invited him on sales trips to Amsterdam, Brussels and Antwerp.

It seemed that at last Vincent was settled, but underneath the front, loneliness was gnawing away at him. He made no friends. HG, now more powerful inside Goupil, was also starting to question whether Vincent, with his gauche weirdness, was right for the job.

WHERE?
SPUISTRAAT,
THE HAGUE, C.1865.

(7)

THEO IN BRUSSELS

"I am so glad that both of us now are to be in the same profession and in the same firm."
Vincent to Theo.

A weird salesman was a contradiction in terms. But to add to Vincent's problems, HG started to question his private life, in particular his regular use of some rather rough prostitutes in the Gueest, The Hague's red light district. He probably used this as a lever to get rid of Vincent for risking the repute of the firm. For the parsonage, where money was very tight, and where Dorus had just had to buy Vincent out at great expense from his military service (he was due to serve fighting rebels in the Dutch colony of Sumatra), a solution was found: Theo would leave school and start to earn by working for Goupil & Cie in Brussels, whilst Vincent would be 'promoted' by being sent to Goupil's wholesale-only (not client-facing) London branch. In a direct parallel to his boarding school years, Vincent was being cast out. To add salt to the wound, Theo impressed in Brussels very quickly, to Anna's delight, a sharp contrast to her disappointment with Vincent. Feeling increasing distance from his parents, Vincent plunged into seeking a closer brotherly union with Theo.

WHO?
THEO VAN GOGH,
C. 1873.

8

PARIS

"When I saw Paris for the first time, I felt above all the dreary misery I could not wave away." Vincent

Once the decision had been made, Cent and HG couldn't get rid of Vincent quickly enough. He was to go to London via Paris. His comments on arriving at the exciting centre of the art world illustrated his very negative state of mind. He was suffering from the blues, he wrote to Theo, and had taken up pipe smoking as a way to cope. In Paris he attended dinners at Uncle Cent's glamorous home, visited the big new Goupil store next to the newly-finished Opéra Garnier and the vast Goupil stockroom, but all with a lack of enthusiasm. He did do the tour of the galleries, soaking up the pictures at the newly-opened Salon, the Louvre and the Luxembourg. Then he was put on a train to Dieppe, crossing the Channel to Brighton and then the train up to London. Vincent was being exiled, away from the centre of the Goupil empire, away from Dorus and Anna and Theo. Worst of all, he was being condemned, as he saw it, to living alone.

WHERE?
PLACE ST MICHEL,
5TH ARRONDISSEMENT,
PARIS, C. 1870.

VINCENT IN THE NETHERLANDS AND BELGIUM 1853-1885

Vincent's father Dorus was a parson, who moved every few years to take up a new position in a new village. This informed Vincent's association with Zundert, his birthplace, Helvoirt (very briefly), Etten and Nuenen. Vincent attended two different schools as a boarder, just far enough away from Zundert to create a painful separation from his family. As an artist, the significant sites were The Hague, where Vincent received art instruction from Anton Mauve, the moorlands of Drenthe, Nuenen and Antwerp.

Key

● Locations of Dorus and Anna Van Gogh's homes (vicarages and parsonages).
● Locations of Van Gogh's schools.
● Locations where Vincent created art.

❶ Zundert
The village where Vincent was born in 1853. He spent much of his childhood here.

❷ Zevenbergen
Vincent's first boarding school, 1864-1866.

❸ Tilburg
Vincent's second school. He boarded in the town. 1866-67.

❹ The Hague
Vincent worked at Goupil & Cie here in 1869.
In 1881 Vincent took some lessons in art here from his cousin, Anton Mauve, before moving to his own apartment at Schenkweg 138, in 1882.

❺ Helvoirt
Vincent was very disappointed when Dorus and Anna moved here in 1870. He stayed with them after being fired from Goupil.

❻ Brussels
Theo worked at Goupil & Cie here from 1873. Vincent moved to Brussels in 1880 and studied briefly at the Academy of Fine Arts.

❼ Etten
Dorus became pastor here in 1875. Vincent moved back to the parsonage here, at intervals, 1875-1881.

❽ Dordrecht
Vincent worked in a bookshop here in 1877.

❾ Amsterdam
Vincent moved here to study to become a pastor in 1877.

❿ The Borinage
Vincent moved to the bleak industrial coal fields here in 1878, where he was a lay preacher. He returned in 1879, when he decided to become an artist.

⓫ Gheel
Dorus had plans to send Vincent to an asylum here in 1879.

⓬ Drenthe
Vincent lived on the bleak moors in 1883.

⓭ Nuenen
Dorus became vicar here in 1883. He died in Nuenen parsonage in 1885.
Vincent had a studio in the village, 1884-85.

⓮ Antwerp
Vincent enrolled at the Royal Academy of Art, and had a studio here, 1885-86.

Vincent in England

England for Vincent initially represented exile. Yet his letters home reveal how London – then the world's biggest metropolis – fascinated him. He decided to make the best of it and make a new start. He worked at the Goupil London branch for two years, soaked up what London's art galleries – the National and Dulwich Picture Gallery included – had to offer, and went on very long walks. He lodged mainly in South London – Greenwich, Brixton and Kennington – but never quite overcame his loneliness. Perhaps as a way to cope, he eventually fell under the spell of the influential preacher, Charles Haddon Spurgeon, and discovered a quasi-religious calling. When later dismissed from Goupil, Vincent, now completely without direction, almost randomly decided to become a teacher. He didn't last long. England proved to be very much an interlude, before Vincent returned home to Anna and Dorus.

①

COVENT GARDEN

"One of the nicest things I've seen is Rotten Row in Hyde Park."
Vincent, letter to the Stockum-Haanebeeks

Every day Van Gogh would commute from his first lodgings in Greenwich, via steamboat, to the Goupil & Cie London branch in Southampton Street, Covent Garden. Unlike The Hague, Brussels and Paris, this branch had no storefront, but was a stockroom where dealers and their runners would grab images for resale. It was Vincent's rather lonely task to select and pack these images. The range in London was smaller than the other branches, and in turn this made the work less interesting: Vincent did not really rate any of the artists whose reproductions he was dealing with. Charles Orbach, the boss in London, invited Vincent to a few social occasions, but the latter's poor English made capitalising on these difficult. Vincent began to feel his isolation keenly, taking lonely tours of the National Gallery and Hyde Park, which at least had the effect of reminding him of nature in the brutal metropolis. He yearned for home.

WHERE?
COVENT GARDEN,
LONDON, C. 1870.

Covent Garden, LONDON.

25

②

87 HACKFORD ROAD

"When [people] don't live up to his too-quick judgement...they become like a bouquet of withered flowers to him." **Anna Van Gogh**

Vincent had started walking from Greenwich to the office – a journey of over 90 minutes – to save the steamboat fare. A search for new lodgings with a shorter walk led him to Hackford Road, Brixton and the home of a widow and her daughter, Ursula and Eugenie Loyer. Vincent had found a surrogate family at last. He wrote back to Anna and Dorus, at their new parsonage at Helvoirt, about his "brother-sister" relationship with Eugenie, and the wonders of an English Christmas. He also threw himself back into his work, was commended and received a raise, which allowed him to send money back home. In his mind he was recovering his relationship with his own family, but they worried that this 'new family' would prove an unstable illusion. Then news came of Theo's transfer to Goupil in The Hague, and of how highly Vincent's old boss, HG, rated his brother. When, after a year in London, Vincent returned to Helvoirt for a reunion with his family, his relationship with Theo had cooled. Then, on his return to London he abruptly left Hackford Road.

WHERE?
87 HACKFORD ROAD (END HOUSE, WITH THE BLUE PLAQUE), BRIXTON, LONDON SW9.

③

395 KENNINGTON ROAD

"Virginity of soul and impurity of body can go together." Vincent to Theo

Vincent's attachment to the Loyers was to become a pattern for the rest of his life: an intense, deeply insecure desire to find a safe berth, a way of cancelling out his demons, followed by rejection. His sister Anna, who had visited him in London, suggested that Eugenie had rejected his advances.

In a depressed state, Vincent moved to Kennington Road and started slackening at Goupil. He also stopped writing home and gave up any attempt at society, except for the company of prostitutes. He resumed his correspondence with Theo, encouraging him to succumb, against Dorus's strict instructions, to the pleasures of the flesh The Hague had to offer.

This was a part of Vincent's first open rebellion against his parents and his uptight sister Anna. The storm eventually passed, and fragile relations were restored, as was Vincent's work ethic. But he now took a different tack, trying to persuade Theo to join him in London. Then Vincent suffered a setback. Goupil was planning to open an exhibition space in London, but Vincent wasn't wanted. He was being transferred to Paris.

WHERE?
395 KENNINGTON ROAD WAS BOMBED FLAT DURING WORLD WAR II. THIS NEIGHBOURING HOUSE IS VERY SIMILAR TO NUMBER 395.

④

THE TABERNACLE

"Our sorrows are all, like ourselves, mortal...They come, but blessed be God, they also go." **Charles Haddon Spurgeon**

Charles Haddon Spurgeon was the most extraordinary Baptist preacher in Victorian London. Every week he filled the purpose-built Metropolitan Tabernacle, around the corner from Vincent's lodgings, with 6000 eager 'disciples'. One of his 'disciples' was Vincent. Ditching his decent into decadence, he now turned with fervour to Spurgeon's message, of following the example of Christ. Vincent changed all his habits, rising and going to bed early and adopting the monastic moto of "prayer and work". The days of visiting prostitutes, for now, were behind him. Letters poured forth back home and to Theo, full of exhortations to piety. His previous literary hero, Michelet, was consigned to the dustbin, along with other romantic and erotic works. Thomas à Kempis's *Imitatio Christi* took its place, and Vincent sent copies to Theo and his sisters. Dorus, initially impressed with Vincent's new found piety, was now worried at his volte face and erratic and obsessive behaviour. Vincent was also seeking out religious images, of scenes from the Bible, of meaningful sunsets and tempetuous seas. Religious zealotry was now his mission.

WHERE?
THE METROPOLITAN TABERNACLE,
SOUTHWARK, SOUTH LONDON.

5

PARIS INTERLUDE

"What a mess he has made...what a scandal and shame!" Dorus Van Gogh

Vincent's tedious religious obsessions came with him to Paris. Nothing could have been less useful to Goupil's business of selling art and pleasure to their *bon viveurs* bourgeois clients. As if to prove the point, Vincent even started questioning Goupil's clients' tastes to their faces. An unauthorised absence for a trip back to his family for Christmas – Goupil's busiest selling season – meant the writing was on the wall. On his return on January 4th he was, to Cent's and everyone else's relief, fired. Vincent dressed things up as though he had resigned with some dignity, and the rest of the family also pretended that it was Vincent's decision. Dorus begged his other brother, Cor, to give Vincent a job in his Amsterdam bookstore. Forewarned, he declined. Dorus and Anna were now concerned that, in the fallout, Theo's burgeoning career would suffer. Vincent knew he had screwed up royally, but couldn't stop himself. He had paranoid episodes, convinced that it was all a conspiracy against him. But the shame he had brought meant he couldn't stay in Paris. He resolved to go back to England. He was 23.

WHERE?
PARISIAN SCENE,
C. 1875.

6

ETTEN

"I have probably done things that...have been very wrong, so I cannot complain."
Vincent to Theo

Just before he left Paris, Vincent received a letter offering him a teaching job at a small boys' school in the English seaside resort of Ramsgate, two hours south of London. On his way, Vincent decided to make a stop to see family in Etten, where Dorus had taken up a position as the vicar a few months previously. Some sort of reconciliation was effected, as Vincent stayed for a few weeks rather than the planned few days. Theo arrived for a visit just before he left, throwing Vincent's failures into sharp relief. It dawned on Vincent that only he was responsible for turning himself into an outcast. From his comfortable berth at the heart of the art world in The Hague, London and Paris, he was on his way to a position at small unknown English school, to start a profession he knew not at all. He had just wasted six years. A tough journey now lay ahead of him.

WHERE?
THE VICARAGE AND CHURCH AT ETTEN,
DRAWN BY VINCENT, 1876.

⑦

RAMSGATE

"I saw from a book that there are 12,000 inhabitants, but I know no more about it."
Vincent on Ramsgate

The school in Ramsgate was a nightmare. Little could have prepared Vincent for the (then) scruffy townhouse in Royal Road that constituted this establishment. Rotten floorboards, broken windows, classrooms squeezed into what had been bedrooms, flea-ridden dorms, this was a scene straight out of Dickens. The man in charge, William Post Stokes, was a charlatan, who was only interested in the fees paid by the parents of the 24 boys. He put Vincent, with his broken English, in charge of most lessons – Maths, French, German and English – and some building maintenance. The only solace was long walks and watching thunderstorms coming in from the sea. Stokes failed to pay Vincent's agreed salary and then, two weeks in, decided out of the blue to move the school to Isleworth on the other side of London. Vincent, surrendering himself to fate, decided to go along with Stokes's plans. He had in any case decided on a future course: he would become, like one of the heroes in the George Eliot novels he was reading, a missionary in London's vast working class suburbs.

WHERE?
6, ROYAL ROAD,
RAMSGATE.

(8)

ISLEWORTH

"I feel heavy depression because everything I have undertaken has failed."
Vincent

Concurrent with his move to Isleworth, Vincent now contacted many of the hundreds of missions in London in search of a position, but to no avail. After a month of searching he gave up. He also moved from Stokes's school to a similar establishment down the road, Holme Court, run by the Reverend Thomas Slade-Jones. Vincent reconnected with an old, religiously-obsessed friend, Harry Gladwell, going on long walks discussing "the Kingdom of God and the Bible." It was on one of these walks that he decided on another new calling: he would become a preacher; surely Dorus would approve. Slade-Jones invited Vincent to preach a sermon on 'The Solace of Christ' at the Methodist church in Richmond, and to teach Sunday School at churches in Petersham and Turnham Green. Anna felt only shame at the rudderless path Vincent had taken, feelings she made abundantly clear when he returned to Etten that Christmas. Why couldn't Vincent be normal and find a normal job?

WHERE?
158 TWICKENHAM ROAD,
ISLEWORTH.
THE LOCATION OF HOLME COURT SCHOOL.

39

VINCENT IN ENGLAND 1873-1876

Vincent initially arrived in England to take up a post at the London branch of Goupil & Cie. During his time there he lodged in Greenwich, Brixton and Kennington, where he became a religious obsessive after hearing the famous preacher T.H. Spurgeon. When he was fired from Goupil, Vincent returned briefly to Holland. In slightly random fashion Vincent decided on a career in England as a teacher. He taught at Ramsgate and Isleworth, before deciding, simultaneously, to become a preacher. Both occupations ended in faliure.

KEY
- First journey to the UK (1873-75)
- Second journey to the UK (1876)

2 RAMSGATE
The site of William Stokes's School, where Vincent taught on his arrival in England in 1876.

3 ISLEWORTH
The William Stokes School moved here in 1876. Van Gogh taught at Holme Court, just down the road.

4 BOX HILL
Charles Orbach, MD of Goupil, and Vincent visited the beauty spot in 1873.

LONDON

1 BRIGHTON
Van Gogh arrived here in 1873 to take up his post at Goupil & Cie.

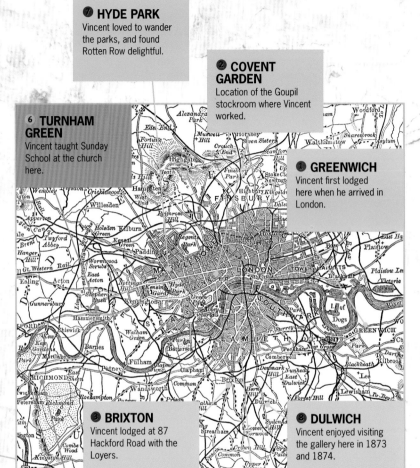

❼ HYDE PARK
Vincent loved to wander the parks, and found Rotten Row delightful.

❷ COVENT GARDEN
Location of the Goupil stockroom where Vincent worked.

❻ TURNHAM GREEN
Vincent taught Sunday School at the church here.

❶ GREENWICH
Vincent first lodged here when he arrived in London.

❸ BRIXTON
Vincent lodged at 87 Hackford Road with the Loyers.

❽ DULWICH
Vincent enjoyed visiting the gallery here in 1873 and 1874.

❺ RICHMOND
Site of Vincent's first sermons.

❹ KENNINGTON
Vincent lived at 395 Kennington Road, not far from the Tabernacle where he went to hear sermons.

Holland Again

Dorus had accepted a position as the parson at Etten, four miles from Zundert, in 1875 and it was here that Vincent retrenched in 1877. Dorus worked hard to find a direction – anything – for Vincent. He managed to find him a job in a respectable bookshop in Dordrecht, but Vincent didn't last long. Vincent then decided he would become a pastor, like Dorus; against his better judgement, Dorus relented, marshalling the family's support in backing Vincent's move to Amsterdam to pursue the studies necessary to get him into university. After endless effort, this proved another failure and Vincent was consigned to becoming a lowly lay preacher in the Borinage – the coal region of western Belgium. It was when he had hit rock bottom here that, somewhat out of the blue, and without any fanfare, Vincent suggested that art would be his true calling.

①

DORDRECHT

"I don't believe there was anyone in Dordrecht who knew him."
Dirk Braat, bookshop owner's son

The last straw was Vincent's latest suggestion that he become a missionary in South America. Dorus and Anna marshalled all their power of argument to persuade him that this was folly. Dorus stated categorically that he could only follow a religious calling if he undertook a proper eight years of study. If not, some other job would have to do. Dorus produced an opportunity (probably arranged by Cent): working for the Blussé and Van Braam bookshop in Dordrecht. Vincent now threw himself with typically obsessive energy into his new role, taking lodgings across the square. But then the old behaviours returned. He began to succumb to depression and loneliness, refusing to mix with any of the staff, going on long solitary walks. He returned to his religious obsessions, which made him the butt of jokes from his fellow boarders. Vincent then had another revelation: he *would* follow Dorus's suggestion and become a pastor like his father. If it meant years of study, so be it.

WHERE?
CENTRAL DORDRECHT,
SOUTH HOLLAND.

②

AMSTERDAM

"How wonderful it would be if he could see his illusion turned into reality."
Lies Van Gogh (sister)

Having originally rejected the idea of studying to become a pastor, Vincent now embraced it with fanatical fervour. Dorus and Anna acquiesced to his plans despite the expense: he would study theology at Amsterdam University. Vincent's poor school record meant he had to undertake preliminary studies prior to taking the entrance exam. But family rallied round. Uncle Stricker, a renowned preacher, offered to guide his studies. Uncle Jan, a rear admiral, offered Vincent lodging in his very comfortable house overlooking Amsterdam harbour. Anna hoped that he would also introduce Vincent to society, having no children of his own. Uncle Cor offered a contribution towards his fees. Only Uncle Cent refused to help. Vincent launched himself frenetically into his studies, from dawn till dusk, copying out endless pages of his Latin, Greek, Maths and Algebra. There was no system to his learning, no analysis. He just crammed information obsessively.

WHERE IS IT?
A VIEW OF AMSTERDAM,
C. 1875

③

THE OUDEZIJDS CHAPEL

"In these [drawings] I can talk...I have found a voice." Vincent

Mauritz Mendes, Vincent's tutor, was beginning to doubt Vincent's abilities. Dorus arrived in Amsterdam to tell Vincent, in his typically wooden fashion, to work harder (as if that were an option). Vincent was close to breakdown and began having suicidal thoughts. But almost imperceptibly, he crossed a rubicon. A service at the Oudezijds Chapel on Sunday June 10th, 1877, in which a new young preacher declared that artists who could express the beauty of nature were doing God's work, had a major impact on him. Theo then announced that he was thinking of becoming an artist. Vincent had a revelation. What if he did the same, as an act of brotherly love? Theo quickly dropped his idea, but Vincent persisted. He at first tried to write about pictures, to capture the 'It', as he put it, that gave a picture its 'truth'. The next step was when Vincent decided to draw, to capture the 'It' in a passage of text, often from the Bible, as an image. He wasn't yet thinking of himself as even an amateur artist, but something had changed.

WHERE?
OUDEZIJDS CHAPEL,
ZEEDIJK,
AMSTERDAM.

4

THE WAALSE KERK

"It's as if he chooses on purpose whatever leads to difficulties." **Dorus Van Gogh**

Vincent was finding his studies harder and more frustrating, and knew deep down he wouldn't succeed at them, so he sought salvation and a future course at the sermons he attended so assiduously. He became very susceptible to preachers. A few days after Dorus visited, a French preacher delivered a sermon at the Waalse Kerk on the misery that capitalism had visited on the industrial poor. Here was Vincent's answer. He would not become an artist, instead he would do God's work by working amongst the underclasses of society. He decided to become a catechist – the most unskilled form of Bible stories teacher, usually of children. Anna was distraught, not least at the shame such a lowly position would bring on the family. Theo visited to try and get Vincent to change his mind. But Vincent's sights were set and he gave up his studies, returning home in shame. Long-suffering Dorus again found him a position, at a ghastly evangelical school in Brussels, but Vincent did not pass the three month trial. His failure was complete.

WHERE?
THE WAALSE KERK,
WALENPLEINTJE,
AMSTERDAM.

⑤

THE BORINAGE

"The miners...are quite black when they emerge into daylight from the dark mines."
Theo to Vincent

Vincent left Brussels suddenly, to the desolate, polluted coalfields and slagheaps of the Borinage region south of Brussels, to take up a post as a lay preacher. Vincent was looking for redemption through adversity, in Christ-like fashion. To the irritation of the miners, whose working conditions made them increasingly militant, Vincent preached sermons on how their suffering made them heroes of God. He quickly lost his audience, so instead searched out the sick and those injured in mining accidents, comforting them in their houses. But soon this didn't satisfy Vincent's inner cravings and so he turned on himself, like a medieval hermit, going to live in an impossibly uncomfortable thatched hut, sleeping on a wooden plank rather than a bed. He barely ate, stopped washing and went barefoot. His religious delusions were of no use to his congregation – to them he was clearly mad – and it all ended inevitably, in Vincent's dismissal. He had no choice but to go home again.

WHERE?
VIEW OF BORINAGE COALFIELDS,
BY VINCENT.

6

GHEEL

"My father called the family for a meeting... in order to have me locked away as a madman." Vincent

Vincent's stay with his parents ended in furious arguments. He left again for the Borinage, but now in a totally nihilistic frame of mind. He lived even more at the extreme, wandering barefoot in the snow, sleeping in barns. He cast everything aside, including his pen for writing letters and his pencil for his sketches. He then, in a suicidal act, set off on a walk to England in freezing conditions. He got as far as Lens before turning back to the Borinage. Dorus had now decided that an asylum was the only place for his son and alighted on the village of Gheel, where lunatics lived relatively calmly amongst the inhabitants. Vincent was now 27, and commital was therefore more complex. At first agreeing to see a doctor, he then ran away, back to the Borinage. He now only maintained contact with Theo. He had reached rock bottom. Then out of the blue a letter to his brother: "I am busy drawing." Vincent had finally decided that art was his true calling.

WHO?
DORUS VAN GOGH,
VINCENT'S FATHER.

A Second New Start

Once Vincent had decided that art would be his destiny, unlike all his other endeavours, he stuck to it. The question was, how would he survive? The answer was Theo, who, from this period onwards, was to provide Vincent with a monthly stipend which covered his rent, clothes, food, drink, fees for models, entertainment (including money for prostitutes), canvases, and a great number of tubes of paint, for the rest of his life. Without Theo, it's likely that Vincent would have sunk without trace. This most extraordinary of brotherly relationships was not without its tensions, but the financial and emotional support, encouragement and advice (ignored more often than not by Vincent) is unique in the history of art. It also produced the amazing, very well-written correspondence which is such a critical part of our understanding of Vincent the artist; Theo kept almost every letter that Vincent wrote. Vincent did not reciprocate; of his letters from Theo, none survives.

1

BRUSSELS

"My aim...to make some drawings that... are saleable as soon as possible."
Vincent to Theo

The switch from preacher to artist happened remarkably quickly, and with the same intensity. Something in Vincent eschewed the need for any sort of instruction. Theo encouraged him, sending him money (establishing a financial dependency) and provided advice on first copying images to improve his skill. Vincent ignored the last, going out to draw from nature from the get-go. After two months in the Borinage, he set off for Brussels with a portfolio full of drawings. He took lodgings near the main station, got himself new clothes, including a suit, and started making connections with other artists, including the well-heeled Anthon van Rappard. To complete the transformation, he applied for a drawing course at the Académie des Beaux-Arts. From beggar tramp and religious fanatic, to urbane artist-about-town in the space of a few weeks: Dorus couldn't believe it, but was relieved enough to promise Vincent one third of his own salary, an allowance of 60 francs a month.

WHERE?
THE NEWLY-BUILT PALAIS DE JUSTICE,
DOMINATING BRUSSELS'S ANCIENT STREETS,
BUILT BETWEEN 1866 AND 1883.

②

THE ACADEMY

"Of one thing he was sure...that I was no artist." **Vincent on his previous boss, HG.**

Vincent became as frenetic about his new role as an artist as he had been in following his religious studies. He acted as if money was no object, spending large amounts on top quality paper and shelling out on models, something most students only did later in their studies. He acquired costumes for his 'character studies' and decided that he must get a proper studio. He also started pressuring Theo to arrange for Goupil in Brussels to support his career. Fearing embarassement, Theo took control by agreeing to cover Vincent's burgeoning expenses. Even so, Vincent now declared that living on 100 francs a month was impossible. At some point he also dropped out of the Academy without explanation. His fellow students had found him strange and annoyingly argumentative, and he made no friends there. The Goupil Brussels branch chose not to help their previously 'weird' employee, despite the family connections. An attempt at a rapprochement with HG failed dismally. Vincent's paranoia began to haunt him again.

WHAT?
STILL LIFE WITH STRAW HAT,
BY VINCENT, 1881.

③

ETTEN

"There has been a change in my drawing, both in the way I set about them and in the result." Vincent to Theo

Vincent retrenched by going home to Etten yet again. The passion for his new calling was, however, undiminished and Vincent would spend many days sketching the countryside around the village. When the weather was too bad he would copy Millet's works, his *Sower* in particular. He also cajoled many villagers to sit for him. Anna and Dorus offered Vincent the use of an outbuilding as his studio and were relieved when Vincent's smart, reassuringly bourgeois artist friend from Brussels, Anthon van Rappard, came to visit. Vincent began to hope for the warmth of a rapprochement with his parents. They, watching the two 'artists' going out sketching together, felt that Vincent should be encouraged. There was no more talk of the asylum. But there was yet no pride in their son, unlike the praise they again showered on Theo on one of his visits from Paris. Vincent now decided on a new way of winning Anna's and Dorus's approval: he would get married.

WHERE?
ROAD IN ETTEN,
BY VINCENT, 1881.

4

KEE VOS

"I hope to leave no stone unturned that might bring me closer to her." Vincent to Theo

With his mind set on marriage, Vincent targeted his cousin, Kee Vos, now 35, as his future partner. He hadn't seen her for three years; in the interim her husband had died, and she was still in mourning, the sort of emotional condition Vincent loved to immerse himself in. She visited Etten in August 1881 and, within a week, without any indication that she had any feelings towards him at all, Vincent had declared his undying love and proposed. Her response was very clear: "Never! No! Never!" In another state of delusion, Vincent did not accept her answer. He spent the next few months inundating Kee, now back in Amsterdam, with letters. A family conflagration was the result, which brought in Uncles Stricker and Cent instructing Dorus to restrain his son. Vincent then corralled Theo to his cause with a battery of correspondence, describing the passion he felt for Kee, and how the family was, as usual, against him. Vincent went to Amsterdam to door-step Kee, without success. Furious arguments with Dorus ensued, with the result that he banished his son from ever stepping in his house again, with the words "God damn you". Vincent was well and truly banished.

WHO?
CORNELIA ('KEE') VOS,
WITH HER SON JAN.

5

THE HAGUE (MAUVE)

"Mauve says 'painting is drawing as well'."
Vincent to Theo

Anton Mauve, Vincent's 42-year old cousin by marriage, was a success. An artist in oils and watercolours, he produced highly commercial images in the manner of the Barbizon school, living a comfortable bourgeois existence in The Hague with his growing family and splendid canal-side studio. For Vincent he represented an ideal. Mauve had kindly agreed to visit Etten to instruct Vincent in "the mysteries of the palette." After Kee's rejections, Vincent turned up in The Hague, renting a room nearby, and received lessons in watercolour from Mauve. Then, after the breakup with Dorus in Etten, Vincent was back again, borrowing money from Mauve, soon spent on renting and decorating a studio nearby. He wrote to Theo asking him for more funds, threatening to borrow again from Mauve if he didn't cough up. Mauve stood outside the fray, but quietly and subtly helped Vincent, allowing him to come to his studio to watch him at work. But, as ever with Vincent, a minor disagreement about methods had whirled up into a furious row, the end result of which was Mauve banning Vincent from coming near his studio again.

WHERE?
MORNING RIDE ALONG THE BEACH,
(AT SCHEVENINGEN),
BY ANTON MAUVE, 1876.

67

6

THE HAGUE (H.G. TERSTEEG)

"This painting of yours will be like all other things you started. It will come to nothing."
Tersteeg to Vincent

In The Hague Vincent also sought out the support of his old boss, Tersteeg ('HG'). The boss of Goupil in the city, his star had risen with the success of The Hague School of painters (including Mauve). Vincent went to reconnect and to borrow money from him, before inviting him to see his work. HG didn't mince his words: Vincent's drawings were unsaleable, he was wasting his time, his figure drawing was a ridiculous obsession, hiding the fact that he couldn't master watercolour. To Vincent, now convinced that he had "the artistic sense in the marrow of my bones", this was treason of a high order. He now demanded that Theo break his relations with HG, that he leave Goupil and join him in the quest to become an artist. Theo instead asked Vincent to calm down in the interests of good relationships. But HG went on the attack again, telling Vincent to give up, get a job and stop sponging off his brother. Vincent's paranoia crept up again: it was him against the World. Yet, far from giving up, he redoubled his efforts.

WHERE?
THE NEW CANAL IN THE HAGUE, C. 1880.
TERSTEEG'S SUCCESS WAS IN SELLING TO THE
HAGUE'S INCREASINGLY WEALTHY MIDDLE CLASSES.

7

SCHENKWEG 138

"One must...go to a prostitute occasionally if there is one you can trust and feel something for." Vincent to Theo

Vincent now set himself up in a modest apartment on the Schenkweg, on the edge of town near the station. He set to work to prove all his detractors wrong and demanded more money from Theo. In his mind he became entitled to it: "a workman is worthy of his wages." Ignoring the entreaties that he paint watercolours and landscapes, he focused mostly on the figure, in dingy greys and browns. He recruited his models from the train station or nearby soup kitchens. Here he was in charge, working at speed, directing poses, with no one to criticise his work. Amongst his models was a pregnant prostitute, Sien Hoornik, and her ageing mother. Their life was in crisis – the sort of emotional chaos that Vincent was so drawn to. Vincent had started an affair with Sien, and was now supporting her and her mother. He was also starting drawing from the nude. Then, in a bombshell letter, he announced to Theo that he intended to marry Sien and bring her future child up as his own.

WHERE?
VIEW OF A NURSERY ON THE SCHENKWEG,
BY VINCENT, 1882.

8

SCHEVENINGEN

"When I paint I feel a power of colour in me." Vincent to Theo

Shortly after meeting Sien, Vincent was in hospital with a nasty case of gonorrhea. Theo had decided that Sien was proof that Vincent really had lost his mind. He warned his brother that when Dorus found out, he could once again seek to have Vincent committed. Theo did not mention his anger that he was clearly now supporting Vincent, Sien and her mother. When Sien gave birth to a boy, Vincent was deluded that seeing him with his 'family' would reconcile even Dorus. Doubts crept in when Tersteeg visited and saw the family tableau: "Have you gone mad?" he demanded. When Theo visited that August he was resolute: If Vincent wanted to continue receiving funds, he must forget the marriage idea. Not only that: Vincent had also to drop his unsaleable black and white figures, and paint landscapes and in colour. Vincent tried, and discovered he really *could* paint. He plunged into the new medium, completing twelve canvases, many of the Scheveningen beach near The Hague, in the month after Theo's visit.

WHERE?
THE BLEACHING GROUND AT SCHEVENINGEN,
BY VINCENT, 1882.

⑨

THE HAGUE

"I feel less passion for her than I did for Kee Vos last year." Vincent, about Sien.

Just when he seemed to be striking a bright new path with intensity, Vincent somehow then perversely gave up and did the opposite, maniacally. He now became obsessed with English monochrome heart-wrenching images of London's underclasses. He renounced paint and was back working with charcoal and pencil. He also imagined he could find work as an illustrator, for publications using the new photogravure presses. His vision that he would be welcomed with open arms received a reality-check when one publication, *The Graphic*, revealed they had over 2,000 illustrators on their books. And family life was taking its toll. Sien's very crude relatives began to irritate him, she was focused on the baby, they had stopped having sex, and he was beginning to suspect he was being used. He then came up with a crazy plan to turn the apartment into a soup kitchen, which would allow him an endless stream of hungry, impoverished models. Theo was appalled when he found out, and tried to steer Vincent in the direction of the rising popularity of the colour-filled impressionists, to no avail. Vincent responded by launching a quest to find the blackest black.

WHERE?
THE PUBLIC SOUP KITCHEN,
BY VINCENT, 1883.

To the Moors and Back

Having half agreed to give Sien up – "I need time to decide," he told Theo – Vincent picked Drenthe, the remote moorland region to the north of the Netherlands, as a place to escape and his next artistic destination. In this he was inspired by Mauve and van Rappard: both had travelled there independently to paint. On his way he stopped at Nuenen to reconcile with his family (Dorus had been appointed parson there in 1882). Vincent stayed in Drenthe for three months, producing a good body of work: drawings, watercolours and paintings. During his stay he repeatedly begged Theo to join him in a joint artistic endeavour, but returned to Nuenen when Theo declined the impossibly impractical offer. Vincent now landed back with Dorus and Anna. They offered him a studio attached to the parsonage to support his endeavours, but this period was characterised by endless rows with Dorus, and, in his upstanding parents' eyes, unsuitable and shaming liaisons in the small village, both possibly contributing to Dorus's fatal heart attack in 1885.

1

HOOGEVEEN

"Come brother, come and paint with me on the heath." Vincent to Theo

Theo again made it clear that any future call on funds would mean Vincent leaving Sien. Vincent gave in, deciding to go and paint in some desolate wilderness. He picked Drenthe, the northernmost region of The Netherlands, all bleakness and moorland, seven hours by train. Van Rappard had been there, which helped Vincent with his decision. He picked Hoogeveen as it was on the trainline, but soon discovered how charmless it was. Yet he found beauty amongst the peat-gathering peasants and in the "vast sun-scorched earth...against the lilac hues of the evening sky." Signficantly, after a year of perverse reluctance, he started to paint again, vowing to Theo that 100 serious studies would soon be completed. But soon his isolation and loneliness enveloped Vincent. The locals rejected him. He longed for Sien. He had few funds left (he had given Sien a chunk on departing) and was running out of paint. He began to blame Theo for his plight. Then in September Vincent suffered his first recorded psychotic episode. He then begged Theo to abandon everything, and to join him on the blasted heath.

WHERE?
PEAT BOG, DRENTHE.
BY VINCENT, 1883.

②

VEENOORD

"Imagine the silence, the peace!"
Vincent to Theo

Plunging further into the challenge of isolation, Vincent now headed
16 miles to Veenoord, by barge. He had a new injection of funds and
paints from The Hague. His letters to Theo were obsessive: Theo *must*
give everything up and join him. Vincent treated these entreaties like a
mission, ignoring the central problem: money. But his facility with paint
was increasing – he recognised that this was the medium with which to
capture the storms over the flat, desolate, treeless landscape. As he
painted, he was, we can see with the benefit of hindsight, discovering
a new direction for art, one where the paint itself expressed rather than
represented. Vincent wasn't yet articulating this, and no one else was yet
seeing it, and especially not Theo. Vincent started attacking his brother
for not joining him on the moors. Theo retorted to the effect: who on
earth do you think is supporting you and our parents? Why do you think
I'm still at Goupil?

3

NUENEN

"It wasn't as lonely on the heath as it is in this house." Vincent to Theo

When simple pleas to join him in his art didn't work on Theo, Vincent then threatened to commit suicide, to refuse his funds. This proved an empty threat, but now he tried a different tack: he would go and impose himself on their parents again. After a vicious exchange of letters, Vincent suddenly left the moors in November, walking the 16 cold miles to the nearest station. In his portfolio he had many images of imprisonment, reflecting his state of mind. As soon as he arrived at the parsonage at Nuenen, the rows began. Vincent demanded of his father that he admit that all of Vincent's hardship over the past two years was his fault. Weeks of three and four hour arguments ensued. Dorus offered money, a studio, Anna even stopped criticising; but for Vincent this wasn't enough. He threatened to marry Sien again, blaming Dorus and Anna for his failure with Kee. He began frequenting – and painting – lonely loom workers' houses, much to bourgeois Anna's distress. Only when Anna had an accident stepping out of a train did Vincent relent. He loved helping the helpless and Vincent became her nurse and carer.

④

KERKSTRAAT

"There needs to be more gusto in my life if I am to get more brio into my brush."
Vincent to Theo.

Eventually Vincent and Theo resolved their differences and came up with a new 'arrangement': Theo would send 150 francs a month and Vincent would send Theo work in exchange; thus the fiction that Theo was buying Vincent's work was established. Theo had shown some of Vincent's work in Paris, but found no buyers. A proposed visit from Vincent's artist friend van Rappard, spurred Vincent to properly play the role of artist and with Theo's funds he established himself at a studio in Kerkstraat, next to the Catholic church. There was a further motivation. Vincent wanted to use hookers again, hard to do at The Vicarage. The new studio also made it easier with models, including the 29 year-old Gordina de Groot, with whom, as he put it, he 'flattened the corn' (and who he weirdly insisted on calling 'Sien'). Vincent was reinventing himself (inspired by the eponymous hero of *The Sin of Abbé Mouret*, by Zola), as a sharp, amoral man of action, whether with art or women. He also started networking amongst nearby Eindhoven's amateur artists, and earnt some money mentoring a few. It seemed that Vincent was on the up.

WHO?
GORDINA DE GROOT,
BY VINCENT, 1885.

5

MARGOT BEGEMANN

*"The man of faith, of energy, of warmth...
wades in...he violates, he 'defiles'."*
Vincent

But poor Vincent screwed up again, this time literally, with the spinster virgin 43-year old daughter of the Begemanns, the wealthiest Protestant family in Nuenen and good friends of Dorus and Anna. Margot Begemann met Vincent when she came to help Anna after her accident. They soon started seeing each other secretly, knowing their relationship would be frowned upon. They met for seven months, before Vincent was caught *in flagrante* on the Begemann's sofa whilst the family were out. Outrage ensued. Vincent said he would marry Margot, but her family decided on banishment. On the night before she was dispatched to Utrecht, she met Vincent in a field and revealed she had taken strychnine. Vincent managed to get her to vomit before getting her to a doctor. Vincent's confidence, his bravura persona, now collapsed, and he turned on his father as the root cause. He also started arguing with Theo again, and rejected the move to colour. His work was once more turning to perversly unsaleable dingy blacks.

WHERE?
PEASANT VILLAGE AT DUSK,
(VIEW OF NUENEN OUTSKIRTS),
BY VINCENT, 1884.

86

6

KERKSTRAAT 2

"I cannot give up the studio...and they cannot demand I leave the village." Vincent

Vincent had always viewed his friend van Rappard as an artistic fellow traveller. However, the moment van Rappard found success (he won a silver medal at a London show), weird, uncouth Vincent was dropped. His response was to go on a manic programme of portrait painting. He seemed to pick many of his models for their ugliness and he set a target of 50 portraits in one month. It's likely that he also slept with some of his subjects, describing them ambiguously "as fair and clean as some whores." Vincent started to get a reputation around Nuenen, not helpful to his father the pastor. Dorus was buckling under the stress of having his impossible son around. Theo tried to suggest to Vincent that he move to Eindhoven, but he would have none of it. Theo was now thinking that Vincent should be persuaded that art should be a pastime, not an end in itself. He implored Vincent to mend fences with Dorus, to which Vincent replied "I do not much care for deathbed reconciliations". He got his wish. Dorus Van Gogh dropped dead from a heart attack, aged 63, on March 27th, 1885. It was Vincent's 32nd birthday.

WHAT?
STILL LIFE WITH OPEN BIBLE, BY VINCENT, 1885.
(THE BIBLE SUGGESTS DORUS; THE CANDLE IS EXTINGUISHED
BEFORE ITS TIME. THE WELL-THUMBED PAPERBACK NOVEL, VINCENT.)

Back to the City

Dorus's death made Vincent *persona non grata* in Nuenen. He now effected a dramatic change of direction. Henceforth, he decided, his stamping grounds would be Amsterdam, Antwerp (where he signed up at the Royal Academy) and Paris. Vincent landed on Theo unannounced and the two brothers ended up living together (a time sadly not recorded in correspondence, for obvious reasons). Vincent enjoyed life in Paris to the full, even reprising his previous role as an art dealer, working together with the now very successful and influential brother. Theo, of course, was still paying for everything.

1

THE RIJKSMUSEUM

"When looking at pictures...one must... admire what is beautiful."
Vincent

After Dorus's death, Vincent's sister Anna took charge: Vincent would simply have to leave, she declared unsentimentally. There were other reasons to go also: the Catholic priest, concerned that many models were posing naked for Vincent, banned them from going to the Kerkstraat studio. Gordina was also pregnant. Even Vincent recognised it was time to make himself scarce. He headed to Amsterdam, where he spent a heady three days ensconced in the newly opened Rijksmuseum. He found parallels between Frans Hals's use of black and his own. He admired Rembrandt's cadavers and his use of ochres and browns. Above all he identified with the brio and speed with which these Dutch masters painted. This was about admiring paint, not about the accurate depiction of a subject. It was a revelation; Vincent now planned to 'explode' paint on his canvases, in a frantic rush that captured all he was feeling. Instinctively, Vincent knew he was creating a new kind of art.

WHERE?
THE RIJKSMUSEUM,
AMSTERDAM,
SHORTLY AFTER IT OPENED IN 1885.

2

ANTWERP

"What they say about Antwerp is true: the women are all handsome." Vincent

Vincent had left Nuenen surruptitiously, to avoid having to pay the due rent on the studio. He decided to move to Antwerp with its sailors' bars, bustle and prostitutes. It was a blessed relief from Nuenen's uptightness and censorious villagers. He dreamt up a new, delusional scheme. He could get whores to pose for him for modest sums: they could use their portraits to attract clients. His sitters of course wanted bright colours, and Vincent began to use cobalt blues, carmine reds, vermillion and lilacs. But the scheme didn't work – whores needed up-front cash and, for publicity, preferred the new art of photography. Vincent was once again wasting Theo's money on paid models, paying them again to also sleep with him. Worse, he confessed to Theo, he had now contracted syphilis, with the attendant sore gums, loosened teeth and the dreaded mercury treatment. Side effects included hair loss, anaemia and weak eyesight, with tell-tale frothing at the mouth and large ulcers. To add to Vincent's depression, none of his pictures sold. Theo, dreading another Sien episode, told him he had to leave the city.

WHERE?
ANTWERP HARBOUR,
IN 1885.

3

ANTWERP ACADEMY

"I...no longer care what people say about me or about my work."
Vincent to Theo

In almost child-like fashion, Vincent now begged Theo to let him stay. With another volte face – he had said he would never go to an art school again – he enrolled at drawing classes at the prestigious Royal Academy of Art. He was a changed man, he told Theo, one who *would* listen to instruction – even accepting drawing from plaster casts. And he would try and make friends. It didn't go well. Vincent argued fiercely with his tutors, ignoring instructions to draw classical contours and lines, producing instead chunky, big-hipped peasant girls. When his tutors ejected him from their classes, he joined student drawing clubs, but they found Vincent too weird. On entering a drawing contest, the judges recommended he join a class for 10-year olds. His letters to Theo were full of lies, of how all was well. Vincent then had a total breakdown, wandering the streets drunk. When he looked at himself in the mirror he saw the ravages of his syphilis treatment. Not even the hookers would now sleep with him, and money was again running out. Vincent suffered a complete breakdown. It was then that he produced his astounding first self-portrait.

WHAT?
SKULL WITH BURNING CIGARETTE,
BY VINCENT, 1886.

4

MONTMARTRE

"Don't be angry with me for arriving out of the blue." Vincent to Theo

Theo had always resisted his embarrassing brother coming to Paris. After his breakdown, Vincent sent a series of begging letters describing how he was a changed man, how wonderful it would be for the two brothers to be together, how they could save money. Theo stalled, suggesting Vincent should go back to Nuenen. He was ignored. Vincent, leaving a stack of unpaid rent and bills (including his poor dentist's) in Antwerp, landed on Theo unannounced. At least he scrubbed up: a new suit, new wooden dentures and a sharp beard. Theo, resigned, accepted the inevitable and rented a smart new fourth floor apartment in the artists' quarter of Montmartre for them both. Always aware of practicalities, he even hired a kitchen maid. In chameleon fashion, Vincent now adopted a new persona, that of Bel-Ami, from the Maupassant story of a humble outsider who makes it in Paris. He began a series of self-portraits, of Van Gogh the bourgeois artist. He started thinking of how to make his art hyper-commercial: restaurant menus and tourist postcards included. He suddenly started following Theo's advice.

WHERE?
54 RUE LEPIC,
MONTMARTRE.
THE VAN GOGHS' APARTMENT WAS ON THE FOURTH FLOOR.

5

ATELIER CORMON

"The whore is like meat in a butcher's shop... and I sink back into my brutish state." Vincent

Theo had identified the Atelier Cormon, one of the many private art schools that had sprung up in Paris, with its nude models and lax morals, as perfect for Vincent. He pulled the Goupil connection to get him admitted. Vincent again stuck out like a sore thumb, with his thick Dutch accent, amongst the urbane young artists at the school, including the aristocratic Toulouse-Lautrec; Vincent was much older, didn't enjoy their japes, and earnt no respect for his technique. They laughed behind his back at his creations: ridiculous, absurd, and so crude, they thought. He became the object of merciless teasing. Having promised Theo he would stay there for three years, he lasted 12 weeks. Attempts to sell his work – whether paintings (none sold) or illustrations to magazines (same result) – were a resounding failure. In the middle of Paris, Vincent's loneliness returned. It was back to hiring prostitutes to pose for him, many organised by the famed Agostina Segatori (she had posed for Corot and Manet), owner of the renowned Café Tambourin.

WHAT?
RUE DES MOULINS, BY TOULOUSE-LAUTREC
(PROSTITUTES AWAITING A MEDICAL).
LAUTREC PERFECTLY CAPTURED THE LOUCHE
ATMOSPHERE OF THE UNDERBELLY OF 1880'S PARIS.

6

FLOWERS

"Last year I painted almost nothing but flowers." Vincent to his sister Wil

Free from the constraints of the Atelier, Vincent was free to plunge into his obsession since the days of the heath: colour. In 1886 artists in Paris were ablaze with colour theories. Should they follow the impressionists? Or Seurat, with his pointillisme? Obtusely, Vincent had followed old-fashioned Delacroix and his complimentary colours. Difficulties with models and now wishing to explore every different colour theory, Vincent turned to flowers as his subject. Following Theo in admiring the work of Adolphe Monticelli, he created a series of small paintings showing an astonishing range of both colour contrasts and 'harmonies', of dahlias, geraniums, hollyhocks, daisies and lilacs, with thick, almost sculptural brushstrokes. He was thrilled when Segatori agreed to hang some in her Tambourin café (they didn't sell). Vincent was again going against the grain, against Parisian fashions in art, against lightness of touch and Seurat's pointillisme. Back in Rue Lepic, Vincent's perverse character was also starting to stress Theo to the point of illness. He started thinking of ways of asking his brother to leave.

WHAT?
VASE WITH RED AND WHITE FLOWERS,
BY VINCENT, 1886.

(7)

ASNIÈRES

"We have made our peace...I have asked him to stay." Theo to his sister Wil

Just before Theo kicked him out, Vincent changed tack, suddenly. Having obstinately refused to paint outdoors ("bad for my health") or to follow the impressionists for months, Vincent ventured out three or four miles outside Montmartre, to the reaches of the Seine around Asnières. He produced pictures drenched in sunlight, of river barges, rowers, charming riverside restaurants, or the views towards the Butte Montmartre. It turned out that, even whilst vehemently rejecting their techniques, Vincent had in fact studied the impressionists in detail. He now mixed pointillisme, impressionist brushwork and his own take on paint in a single image. There was a new spontaneity to his painting, partly influenced by Signac, who he had met on his excursions. He also returned to painting the highly detailed observations of nature – patches of undergrowth, details of summer wheat, close-ups of saplings – that Theo loved. The brothers made up. But Vincent then saw storm clouds on the horizon: Theo had announced he was thinking of getting married. Vincent fell into a deep depression, and again spoke of suicide.

WHERE?
THE PONT DE CLICHY AT ASNIÈRES,
BY VINCENT, 1887.

8

DEALING AGAIN

"...nowadays one does better looking rich than looking hard up." **Vincent to Theo**

Things were looking bad for Vincent. Theo was off to Amsterdam to propose to the object of his affections, Jo Bonger. Vincent turned his attentions to Agostina Segatori, but she rejected him. Shortly later, her café went bankrupt, and Vincent's pictures were sold as 'a pile of junk'. Theo soon returned from Amsterdam: his suit had been rejected. He now found solace in Vincent's company. They shared the secret of the syphilis they had both contracted. Then, when Goupil decided to start a division searching for the next avant garde art movement, Theo was put in charge of the search, and the Montmartre display space, the Entresol. He needed someone with a deep knowledge of art and artists to help him: who better than Vincent? Vincent took to this new role with alacrity. If the artists he approached thought him strange, they tolerated him for the greater prize of being exhibited at the Entresol. Theo scored a coup when he got Monet to switch to Goupil from his current dealer. Money followed Monet and Theo's reputation grew. This time Vincent rode his coattails without rancour.

WHAT?
SELF PORTRAIT BY VINCENT, 1887.
VINCENT IN DASHING ART-DEALER MODE.

⑨
JAPONISME

"In time your outlook changes, you look on things with a more Japanese eye."
Vincent

Vincent loved his contact with other artists, Lautrec, Pissarro, Guillaumin, Signac and Seurat included. But the one who would now influence him the most was Émile Bernard. Young, full of energy and determined to overturn impressionism, he was pushing for a visual language of colour, of design creating direct sensations. Bernard was influenced by the outrageous new novel by Huysmans, *À Rebours,* the Symbolists, Gothic stained glass and Japanese prints. Vincent, who now saw Bernard as a new object of intense artistic friendship, was hooked, and pursued this new direction with his usual obsessiveness. He scoured Japanese emporia in Paris, he repainted some existing portraits with the brilliance of pure pigments, his new images projected directness and simplicity. The number of brushstrokes was reduced to the point where they could be counted. Given this bright new direction, the connection with dealing and his association with Theo's mission for Goupil and the Entresol, it was very strange that, suddenly, out of the blue, Vincent decided to leave Paris.

WHAT?
OIRAN (AFTER KESAI EISEN),
BY VINCENT, 1887.

The South of France

We don't know why Vincent decided to leave Paris suddenly, in February 1888, but the correspondence between Vincent and Theo now resumed. Vincent headed to Arles, in Provence. It is whilst here, and then in Saint-Rémy, that Vincent created possibly his most memorable and loved works, subsequently recognised as amongst the most significant achievements of nineteenth century art. This was also the time, however, when Vincent's mental breakdowns became debilitating, although he found some release in the realisation that he had probably inherited his mental illness. In recognising his own condition (he was remarkably lucid when describing this to Theo in correspondence, including the famous incident with the ear), Vincent willingly decided that he should become a patient at the Asylum of Saint-Paul de Mausole, in Saint-Rémy.

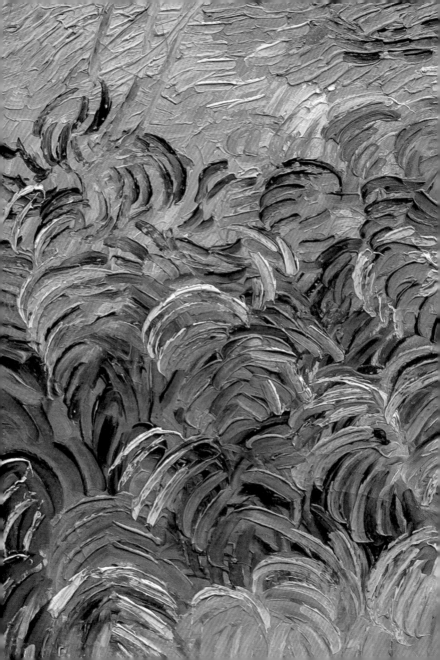

①

ARLES

"I am painting with the gusto of a Marseillais eating bouillabaisse." Vincent

Vincent never explained why he decided on Arles. There were sunnier and warmer places by the coast, or, if he wanted buzz and women, Marseille was more the place. In Arles he took rooms above the Restaurant Carrell. Vincent was disappointed that he hadn't been included in Theo's latest Entresol show (Monet, Pissarro and new boy Gauguin had), but he had offered to submit some of Vincent's paintings to the prestigious fourth Salon des Indépendants. Vincent was newly fired up and the countryside around Arles gave him endless subjects, particularly fruit trees – apricot, plum, pears, apples and peach – and the fabulous cypresses. He started thinking of series of paintings (just as Monet had), thinking all the while of what would sell. But then the loneliness flooded back. And his health – recurring symptoms of syphilis – was on the slide again. Vincent would take to his room for days at a time when the weather was bad, and order his food up from the restaurant. Depressingly, nothing in Paris was selling.

②

THE LANGLOIS BRIDGE

"That mental exhaustion of mine is disappearing." Vincent to Theo

There was something familiar about the canals and bascule bridges around Arles: they had been built by Dutch engineers. They reminded Vincent of home, creating a welter of emotions, of Nuenen, of his father, of his childhood with Theo. Vincent returned to one of these bridges again and again, making various studies from different perspectives, and then painting several different versions. Vincent cooked up a scheme to reconnect with home by sending different versions for his sibblings and old connections in Holland, including Tersteeg. Whilst the paintings that Theo had presented to the Salon didn't sell (they were nearly thrown out at the end of the show), Vincent did receive a review, albeit a critical one. But to even be mentioned was something. But now the old spectre of financial worries returned. Vincent was trying to economise, but was also spending Theo's money too quickly. And, as before, he wasn't getting on with the locals (in letters to Theo describing them as "bores" and "swine"), or his landlord.

WHERE?
THE LANGLOIS BRIDGE,
ARLES TO BOUC CANAL,
ARLES.

③

THE YELLOW HOUSE

"I work...in the full sun...I am as happy as a cicada." Vincent to Émile Bernard

Place Lamartine was at the rough edge of town, next to the station, with an all-night café. It was a park-like enclave used by prostitutes to ply their trade. The faded Yellow House, at the north-east corner, had not been rented for years. It had no electricity, gas or lavatory. But for Vincent it was bliss: one large room downstairs (which could serve as a studio), a tiny kitchen and two bedrooms upstairs. And the rent was cheap. Vincent saw it as a cure for his isolation. He could invite fellow artists to stay, to come and create, a possible starting point for a 'colony' of painters. What if Theo came to stay, when Paris got too much, or Émile Bernard? Or an American artist living nearby, Dodge MacKnight, or failing them, Gauguin? Unfortunately he had no takers. Theo was too ill; Bernard had gone to Brittany (and was trying to get Gauguin to join him). But Vincent was not going to give up; he would concoct a plan to make his dream become reality.

WHERE?
BEDROOM IN ARLES,
(VAN GOGH'S BEDROOM IN THE YELLOW HOUSE),
BY VINCENT, 1888.

④

LES-SAINTES-MARIES

"I have found an absolute Japan in the South of France." Vincent

Vincent made the 30 mile trip to Saintes-Maries-de-la-Mer to paint the renowned little beachside village. He captured the bone-white cottages, but it is for his iconic paintings of the beached fishing boats that the visit is remembered. Strangely, before leaving he left three canvases of the boats on the beach, but returned to the Yellow House in Arles to recreate them indoors, from drawings, on canvas. Inspired by Japonisme, he painted them with black outlines filled with colour. Surely these images would sell in Paris, he enthused to Theo. Vincent then turned again to his illogical pleading to Theo, that he should abandon Goupil and come and be an artist in the Yellow House. As if to emphasize the point, he named one of the boats, one of the sadder blue ones with a black mast, 'Amitié.'

WHERE?
BOATS ON THE BEACH OF LES-SAINTES-MARIES,
BY VINCENT, 1888.

⑤

THE SUNFLOWERS

"Nothing but large sunflowers."
Vincent, on the decorations for Gauguin's room

Vincent had become enamoured of sunflowers whilst in Paris. Now in Arles in early August he returned to them as the flowers were at their fullest bloom in the surrounding fields. He was planning six new paintings of sunflowers to decorate his studio, they would look like "stained glass windows in a gothic church" he wrote to Bernard. But the real motivation was to impress Gauguin. After many entreaties and hesitations, Paul Gauguin had agreed to Theo's suggestion that he join Vincent in Arles. Now Gauguin would arrive to a brilliantly conceived scheme of yellows. When he began painting, he attacked the canvas frenziedly – "like a fencing match." This reached its apogee in one of the images: yellow sunflowers on a yellow-orange table, with a yellow-green background. Vincent was in high spirits and worked frantically to paint the Yellow House interior and then, against his original sunflower plan, covered the bare walls in a cacophony of his other paintings and sketches. He also bought new furniture. Theo, who was paying for all of this, complained loudly at Vincent's extravagance.

6

GAUGUIN

"Shit, shit, shit, everything's yellow!"
Gauguin, on the Yellow House

Everything now hung on the art Vincent and Gauguin would create. But waiting (Gauguin was good at keeping people waiting) was a lonely business and no longer were forays to the Arles brothels a distraction: Vincent now confessed to Theo that he was impotent, a possible side-effect of his syphilis. He had also fallen out with most of the locals. Vincent's depression returned. And then Gauguin turned up, fresh and suntanned from his time in the tropics (Vincent had thought Gauguin was sickly and that he, and the Midi sun, would bring him back to health). Vincent was thrilled. But a few days later came news that Theo had sold a Gauguin painting, *Les Bretonnes*, for a good price. Following a small show in the Entresol, Theo sold a further five pictures. Gauguin was becoming a success. Vincent's plan of a brotherly artistic fight facing adversity lay in tatters. Gauguin did not need him, thanks to his own brother. Sexually voracious, Gauguin had no trouble in finding models to paint and more. He contradicted all of Vincent's artistic theories and, in his manner, didn't hide his disdain for both Vincent and Arles.

WHO?
PAUL GAUGUIN, SELF-PORTRAIT, SENT TO VINCENT IN
ADVANCE OF HIS ARRIVAL AT THE YELLOW HOUSE, 1888.

les misérables
à l'ami Vincent
P Gauguin 88

⑦

THE EAR

"Vincent has been turning very strange..."
Gauguin to Theo

The tensions with Gauguin were causing Vincent many "nervous crises". It wasn't just their arguments, but also the feeling that Gauguin was driving a wedge between him and Theo. Gauguin's success in Paris inevitably meant that he would soon leave Arles, leading to the end of Vincent's dream of an artistic partnership. Gauguin couldn't wait to go, but Theo persuaded him to hang on. He made his move at the worst time – Christmas was always emotional for Vincent – walking out suddenly on 23rd December, the same day that Vincent heard from Theo that Jo Bonger had accepted his marriage proposal. Intense loneliness beconned. Vincent later described what happened as an "attack". We don't know the details, except that Vincent's despair was fuelled by absinthe. After a drinking session he returned to the Yellow House. By the washstand a razor lay waiting. Vincent opened the blade, pulled at his left ear lobe and slashed. Bleeding profusely, he wrapped the severed lobe in newspaper, dressed his wound and went in search of Gauguin at the local brothel. He left the ear with the brothel keeper, to be delivered to Gauguin with the message "Remember me."

WHO?
SELF-PORTRAIT WITH A BANDAGED EAR,
BY VINCENT, 1889.

8

ARLES HOSPITAL

"There's little hope...if he must pass away, so be it." Theo to Jo Bonger

Theo's joy at the prospect of marriage to Jo was somewhat punctured by a telegram from Arles Hospital: Vincent was in danger. Theo rushed down to comfort his brother, but didn't stay long in case an enquiry into the family's medical history should reveal his syphilis (Jo didn't know). For the next few days Vincent was in a manic state, chasing nurses, climbing into bed with other patients in search of comfort, going to wash in a coal bin. His doctors diagnosed 'mental alienation', preparatory to having him committed. But thanks to Frédéric Salles, pastor to the hospital, the diagnosis was reversed and, seven days later, Vincent was back in the Yellow House. Vincent now pretended that nothing serious had happened. He painted two self-portraits for his doctors: in both Vincent looked calm, almost wise. A few days later, however, the police forcibly removed Vincent from his house: 30 of his neighbours had signed a petition declaring him to be crazy, and that they feared for their safety. Vincent was then placed in an isolation cell back in Arles hospital. His only regular visitor was Salles.

WHO?
DR FÉLIX REY, BY VINCENT, 1889.
DR REY, A JUNIOR DOCTOR AT ARLES SPECIALISING IN URINARY TRACT
INFECTIONS, DIAGNOSED "OVEREXCITEMENT" IN VINCENT'S CASE.

9

ASYLUM OF ST PAUL

"He seemed rather excited at the thought of the completely new life that lay ahead of him." **Pastor Salles, letter to Theo**

The doctors treating Vincent couldn't agree on a diagnosis; officially it was 'acute mania with generalised delirium', although Dr Rey now thought VIncent suffered from 'mental epilepsy' – a non-convulsive condition. Theo was indecisive: committing Vincent to an asylum was a shameful step, but having him in Paris would be worse. Vincent's mother also rejected the idea that he should be close to her near Breda. Vincent was totally opposed to going to an asylum, but a few days later followed Salles's suggestion and decided on a small Catholic establishment in St Rémy, 15 miles from Arles. It was ideal. Residents were kept an eye on, but had a relaxed regime and were encouraged to spend time in the extensive gardens, with their tree-shaded walkways. Vincent at last found serenity. His fellow patients were eccentric but civilised and the temptations of absinthe and the brothel were out of reach. His doctors were kindly and, at last, Vincent began to accept he had a condition, possibly hereditary: it wasn't his fault. A huge weight of guilt was lifted from his shoulders.

WHERE?
VIEW OF THE ASYLUM OF ST PAUL,
ST RÉMY-DE-PROVENCE.

VINCENT IN FRANCE 1886-1890

Vincent arrived unannounced in Paris in 1886, and for the next couple of years he and Theo lived together in Montmartre. Vincent painted landscapes in Montmartre and Asnières as well as many flower paintings whilst in Paris. In 1888 Vincent left Paris suddenly, for the Arles in south of France. This is where he created many of his most memorable works, but also where he suffered relapses and 'attacks' (such as the episode with the ear). After his work was finally recognised, in 1889 and 1890, Vincent moved to Auvers, where he died on 27th July, 1890.

AUVERS-SUR-OISE
Vincent moved here in 1890, to be near Theo in Paris. he died at the Ravoux Inn after being shot, on July 27th/28th, 1890.

PARIS

¹ ARLES
Vincent lived here from 1888, first above the restaurant Carrell, then at the Yellow House.

² SAINTES-MARIES-DE-LA-MER
Vincent painted here in June 1888, including a few seascapes and beach scenes.

³ ST RÉMY
Location of the Asylum of St Paul, where Vincent lived after his breakdown in 1889.

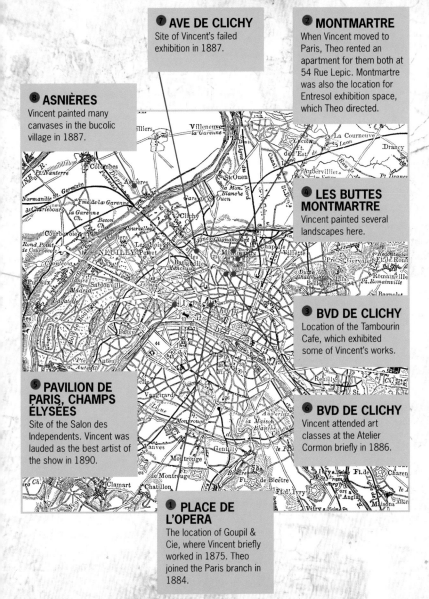

⑦ AVE DE CLICHY
Site of Vincent's failed exhibition in 1887.

② MONTMARTRE
When Vincent moved to Paris, Theo rented an apartment for them both at 54 Rue Lepic. Montmartre was also the location for Entresol exhibition space, which Theo directed.

⑧ ASNIÈRES
Vincent painted many canvases in the bucolic village in 1887.

④ LES BUTTES MONTMARTRE
Vincent painted several landscapes here.

③ BVD DE CLICHY
Location of the Tambourin Cafe, which exhibited some of Vincent's works.

⑤ PAVILION DE PARIS, CHAMPS ÉLYSÉES
Site of the Salon des Independents. Vincent was lauded as the best artist of the show in 1890.

⑥ BVD DE CLICHY
Vincent attended art classes at the Atelier Cormon briefly in 1886.

① PLACE DE L'OPERA
The location of Goupil & Cie, where Vincent briefly worked in 1875. Theo joined the Paris branch in 1884.

131

Recognition

It is the intensely poignant tragedy of Vincent's life that recognition, when it came, was just too late for him to really cope. Any other artist would have jumped on the opportunities presented by the glowing review by the brilliant critic, Albert Aurier, in the *Mercure de France*, and the way his paintings were fêted at the Salon des Indépendants in 1890. But Vincent instead became withdrawn. He did at least leave Saint-Rémy and headed north to be near Theo at Auvers-sur-Oise, some 20 miles outside Paris. As in Provence, Vincent was hugely productive here, creating stunning images of the picturesque village and of his doctor, Dr Gachet.

It was utterly shocking that the end, when it came on July 27th, 1890, happened in the middle of a typically busy day painting in the fields. Exactly what precipitated the events of that fateful afternoon remain shrouded in mystery. The effervescence, the energy, the unmatched joy of paint on canvas from this period, leaves us devoid of words when faced with Vincent's tragic end. His art, however, only grows in stature, touching the lives and emotions of tens of millions the world over.

1

STARRY NIGHT

"I am always frightened when you work like one posessed." **Theo to Vincent**

With his newly found serenity, Vincent could concentrate on painting. He was given a large room to set up his studio near the garden on the ground floor. He painted what he called 'little things': the details of ivy on a tree trunk, a garden bench, a tiny moth and a bed of irises. He associated his favoured new colours – lilacs and lavenders – with the serenity of Saint Paul. His condition was so improved, that Vincent was allowed out into the enclosed field of the asylum, where he painted wheat fields against the violet Alpilles hills, and then further afield, accompanied by a warden, to paint orchards, olive groves and his wonderful cypresses. Vincent's paintings now depicted a sense of divine harmony, none more so than in his starry night images. He would sketch his subject – the valley and village – during the day and, forbidden as he was from going out at night, the sky as seen from the barred window of his room, transformed by visions in his imagination.

WHERE?
THE NIGHT SKY OVER ST RÉMY,
STARRY NIGHT, BY VINCENT, 1889.

2

RELAPSE

"I had been working quite calmly...when suddenly, without reason, I once again became confused..." **Vincent to Theo and Jo**

Vincent was to suffer another wave of attacks in August, probably prompted by the news that Jo Bonger was pregnant, as well as the stirring up of old memories on a trip to Arles. He was now confined again to the asylum and found solace in creating paintings inspired by Millet. Then, in September, he was back to normal, and returned to painting olive groves outside the asylum walls. This latest set of paintings inspired Theo to praise them, and he also had news: Vincent's work would be reviewed in the Dutch art magazine *De Portefeuille*. Enquiries also were starting to come in from people who had seen *Starry Night* and one of the *Irises* at a group show. Theo was now raising the prospect that Vincent could come and live in Auvers, near them in Paris. But then Vincent had another series of attacks, probably brought on by the melancholia he always felt around Christmas. This time the attacks were more serious: no one could get through to him and this time not only could he not paint, he couldn't read or write.

WHERE?
OLIVE GROVE, OUTSIDE ST RÉMY,
BY VINCENT, 1889

③

THE MERCURE DE FRANCE

"Your article...surprised me a good deal..."
Vincent to Albert Aurier

The *De Portefeuille* article got Vincent noticed. In Paris the dealer Tanguy put some of his paintings in his window and people were coming to take a look. One of these was Albert Aurier, a 24 year-old happening art critic, enthusiast of Huysmans's *À Rebours* and the Symbolists. Aurier spotted something electrifying in Vincent's art and in his tragic backstory: here was a new art viscerally connected to sensation and emotion, and from a cerebral epileptic, a quality identifiable with genius. Vincent fitted the idea of real creativity as a sort of 'attack'. Aurier decided he would feature Vincent in the first issue of his new journal, the *Mercure de France*. The article celebrated Vincent as a genius, who had created a new art which connected directly to the senses, 'orgiastically'. When the *Mercure* appeared it created a sensation. The whole Parisian art world began talking about 'Vincent'. Theo had already arranged for Vincent to be featured in the Vingtistes show in Brussels. When it opened the critics showered Vincent with praise. Vincent didn't know how to react. It felt strange, and now he felt unworthy, a fraud.

WHO?
THE ART CRITIC ALBERT AURIER, C. 1889.

④

ARLES AGAIN

"Everything that reminds him of the past makes him sad and melancholy."
Theo to Anna Van Gogh

The new attention sent Vincent into his shell. He was now terrified of the embarrassment he would cause his family, with the public revelation that he was in an asylum. He was concerned about being identified with the 'degenerate' symbolists by his family. Even the fact that Theo had named his new son 'Vincent' caused him pain: he was unworthy. He took solace by plunging into a picture of almond blossom, intended for his nephew.

He then decided on a trip to Arles, but somewhere on the way he had another attack and was found the next day in an amnesic state wandering the streets, not remembering who he was. Vincent was returned to his room at St Rémy, suffering from hallucinations. He barely noticed his 37th birthday. He didn't go anywhere for two months. Then suddenly, he was fine again, and determined to leave St Rémy: he would take Theo up on his suggestion to go to Auvers, where a Dr Gachet would look after him.

WHAT?
ALMOND BLOSSOM, BY VINCENT, 1890.

5

LE SALON DES INDÉPENDANTS

"Ten paintings that bear witness to a rare genius." The Mercure de France

Whilst Vincent was locked in his depressive cycle in St Rémy, Theo had been busy. He had selected ten paintings of Vincent's to hang alongside many of the greats – Lautrec, Signac, Seurat, Pissarro and Guillaumin. When the show opened in March, there was a flood of visitors, many keen to see the 'genius' identified by Aurier. The press, and no less a figure than Monet, decided Vincent's pictures were the best in the show. Even the prickly Gauguin wrote to Vincent to express how brilliant his pictures were. And, perhaps most significantly, the first financial fruits of Vincent's labours were being deposited in Theo's bank account. After all the pain, the angst, the hundreds of pictures, the endless tubes of paint expended, the dismissal of his work by family (in particular his mother Anna, but also by Theo), critics, friends, fellow artists, and the locals treating him like a madman, at his moment of Parisian triumph, Vincent wasn't there. But on May 16th, Vincent finally left the asylum at St Rémy bound for Paris. The asylum doctor, Dr Peyron, had written 'cured' on his medical record.

WHERE?
PAVILION DE LA VILLE DE PARIS,
THE LOCATION FOR THE SALON DES INDÉPENDANTS,
CHAMPS ÉLYSÉES, PARIS.

143

6

AUVERS-SUR-OISE

"I see no happy future at all."
Vincent, on Auvers, to Theo

Vincent spent only three days in Paris before heading for Auvers. He had
been shocked to see how unhealthy Theo looked, but was charmed to
see so many of his pictures hanging in the apartment. Yet in Auvers he
felt the old loneliness pressing in on him again. He was free to wander
at will, and commented on how lovely the countryside was. But he was
less impressed (even though they became friends) with Dr Gachet, who
was entrusted with keeping an eye on Vincent. The old delusions started
coming back: the solution to his loneliness would be to persuade Theo,
Jo and his nephew to come and live with him. He would paint a series of
pictures, starting with Dr Gachet, to show how Auvers was *the* place. He
then painted the villas, the vineyards, the gardens, the thatched cottages
and the gothic church as subjects. Dr Gachet, rather glibly, declared that
Vincent was totally recovered, inspiring Theo to make a quick day trip to
see him. Vincent now redoubled his efforts to persuade Theo, culminating
in a big canvas of the house of the artist Charles Daubigny, the hero of
the Barbizon School that Theo loved.

WHERE?
HOUSES AT AUVERS,
BY VINCENT, 1890.

7

LONELINESS

"I am giving my canvases my undivided attention." Vincent to Theo, from his last letter

Auvers was not the paradise which Vincent had painted. Without friends (not even Pissarro, who was six miles away, bothered to visit), with Theo clearly not planning to move, and with the locals reacting badly to Vincent's awkward manner and insistent requests that they pose for him, Vincent began to retreat into feelings of remorse about his past. He was highly strung, terrified that he would suffer another attack. He did attract the attention of local teenage boys, who nicknamed him 'Toto' and teased and played pranks on him mercilessly after plying him with drink. Vincent accepted this as the price for companionship, particularly with René Secrétan, a 16-year old from Paris who spent his holidays at Auvers. Vincent's sense of insecurity was exacerbated by Theo's news from Paris: he was planning to leave Goupil and go out on his own, supported by Jo's brother Andries, and he planned to move his family to the same building as Andries's. The two happy families would strengthen and get closer to each other: Vincent was surplus to requirements.

WHO?
SELF-PORTRAIT, BY VINCENT (POSSIBLY HIS LAST), 1889.

8

A QUIET END

"Goodbye for now, keep well and good luck with business, etc." Vincent, signing off what would be his last letter to Theo

Vincent redoubled his efforts with his paintings as an entreaty to Theo to move to Auvers. He sent Theo what would be his last letter on July 23rd, 1890. Four days later he spent the morning painting, then returned to the Ravoux Inn for lunch. He left again with easel, canvas and paints to go and paint in the countryside, following his normal routine. As evening fell, the diners on the terrace of the Ravoux Inn saw Vincent staggering back, without easel or canvas, clutching his stomach. He went straight up to his room. When Gustave Ravoux went to check on him, Vincent was lying on his bed bleeding. "I have wounded myself" he said. A Dr Mazery was called and he identified a gunshot wound. Dr Gachet then appeared and spoke to Vincent, still lucid, but could get no hard information out of him. The doctors dressed the wound and Gachet wrote, rather than telegrammed, to Theo in Paris. Theo arrived on the 28th to find Vincent in pain, but smoking a pipe. The brothers talked at length. Then Vincent started falling in and out of consciousness. He died that night, at half-past midnight, with Theo by his side.

WHERE?
THE RAVOUX INN, AUVERS, AT DUSK.
VINCENT DIED IN HIS UPSTAIRS ROOM.

9

WHO KILLED VAN GOGH?

"[It is]...premature to rule out suicide."
Leo Jansen, director, Van Gogh Museum

Suicide is the standard explanation of what happened to Vincent on July 27th, 1890. But the events surrounding that fateful afternoon raise serious questions over what is, ultimately, an assumption. Vincent had often spoken of suicide, but always by drowning. There was no note, no apology to Theo. His recent paintings had been full of vivacity. It is strange that he should be busy painting in the morning, have lunch and then go out to paint again as normal, had he intended suicide. Vincent had never posessed a gun, didn't know how to use one and they weren't easy to come by in Auvers. The gun was a 'peashooter' junior pistol – strange. And Vincent had been shot in the lower stomach – not the natural spot to ensure a decisive end. Neither gun nor Vincent's painting gear was found. To Dr Mazery Vincent had said "Do not accuse anyone. It is I who wanted to kill myself", a strange form of words. Stephen Naifeh and Gregory White Smith advanced an alternative, convincing, theory in 2011, that Vincent was the victim of a teenagers' prank gone awry. Shortly after the shooting René Secrétan left town. When the Auvers police did an inventory, his was the only gun missing.

WHERE?
FIELDS OUTSIDE AUVERS, BY VINCENT, 1890.
PAINTED SHORTLY BEFORE HIS DEATH.

CREDITS

Photo credits below are listed in section and page title order. Graffito wishes to thank all individuals and picture libraries who helped track down sometimes elusive images.
In credits below, Alamy = Alamy Stock Photo.

Art Director:
Karen Wilks
Managing Editor:
Anthony Bland
Research Editor:
Serena Pethick

A note on the author.
Of Anglo-Spanish parentage, Ian Castello-Cortes grew up in South America and Cambridge, England. He is a publisher and writer with a particular interest in contemporary counter-cultures. Ian studied Modern History at Oxford University.

First published in the United States of America by Gingko Press, August 2019.
Gingko Press, Inc.: 2332 Fourth Street, Suite E, Berkeley, CA 94710, USA.
Gingko Press Verlags GmbH: Schulterblatt 58, 20357 Hamburg, Germany.
Published under license from Graffito Books, UK
© Graffito Books Ltd, 2019. www.graffitobooks.com
ISBN: 978-3-94333-039-7
All rights reserved.
Printed in China.